Pretty
POND LIFE
Coloring Book

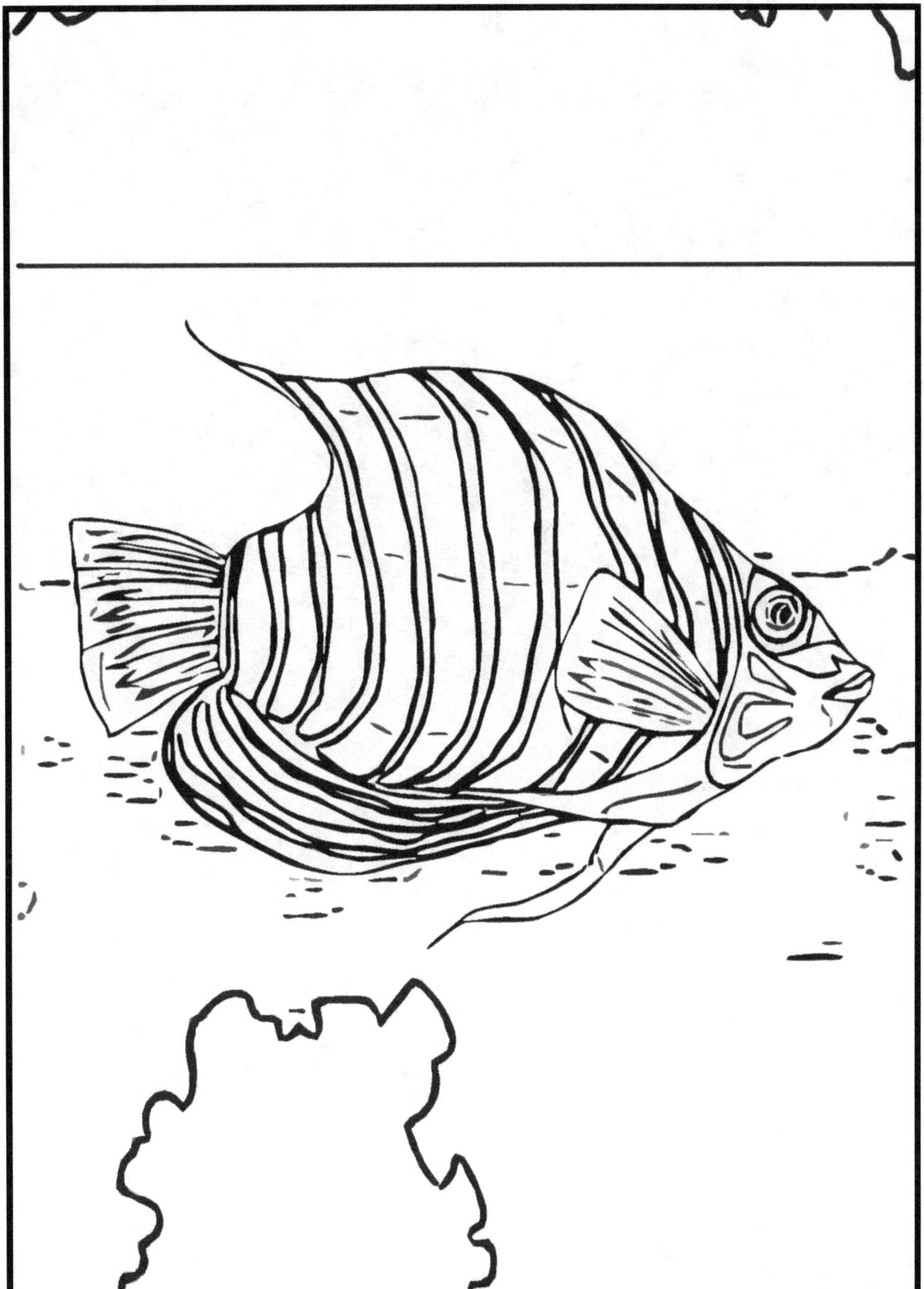

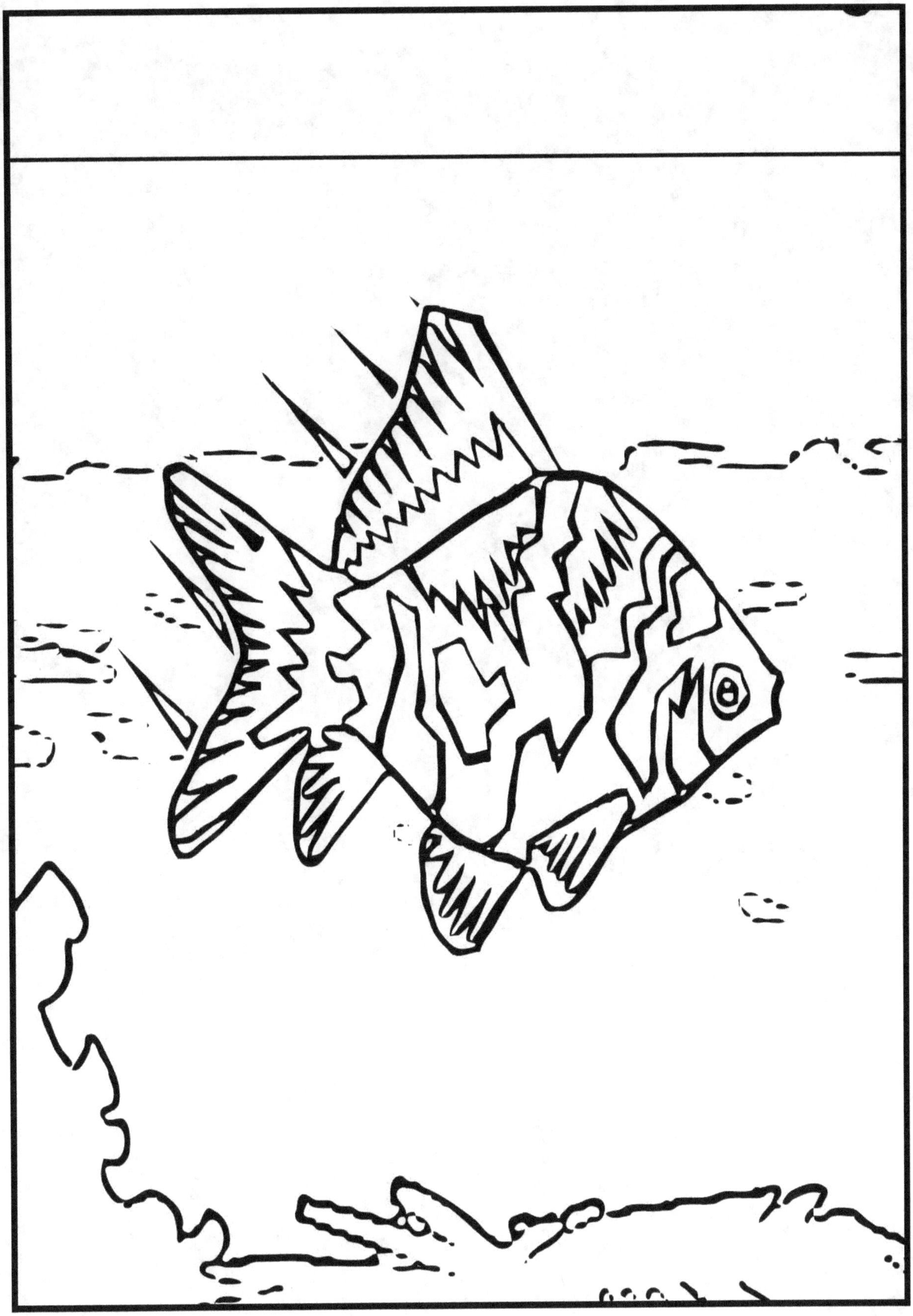

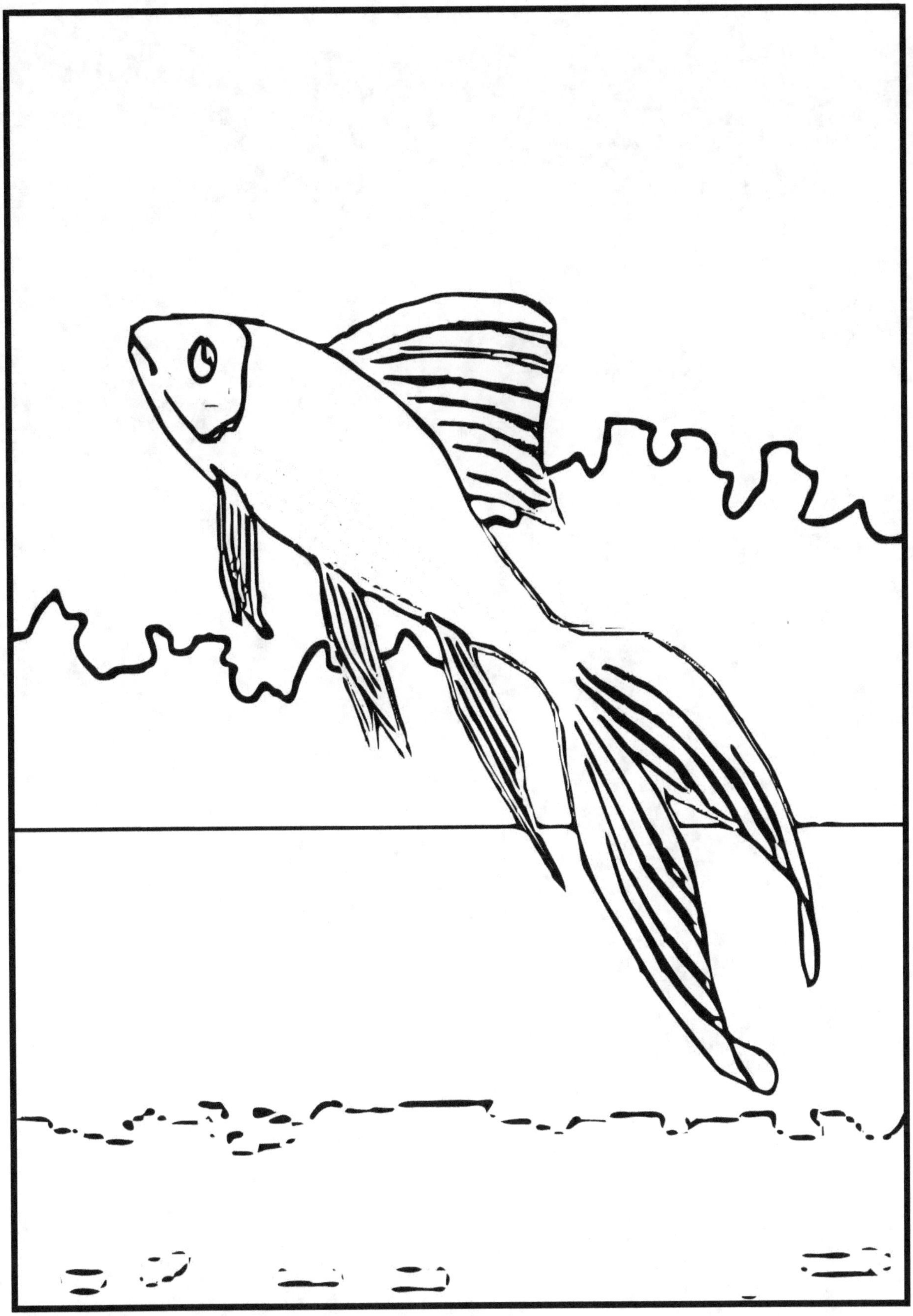

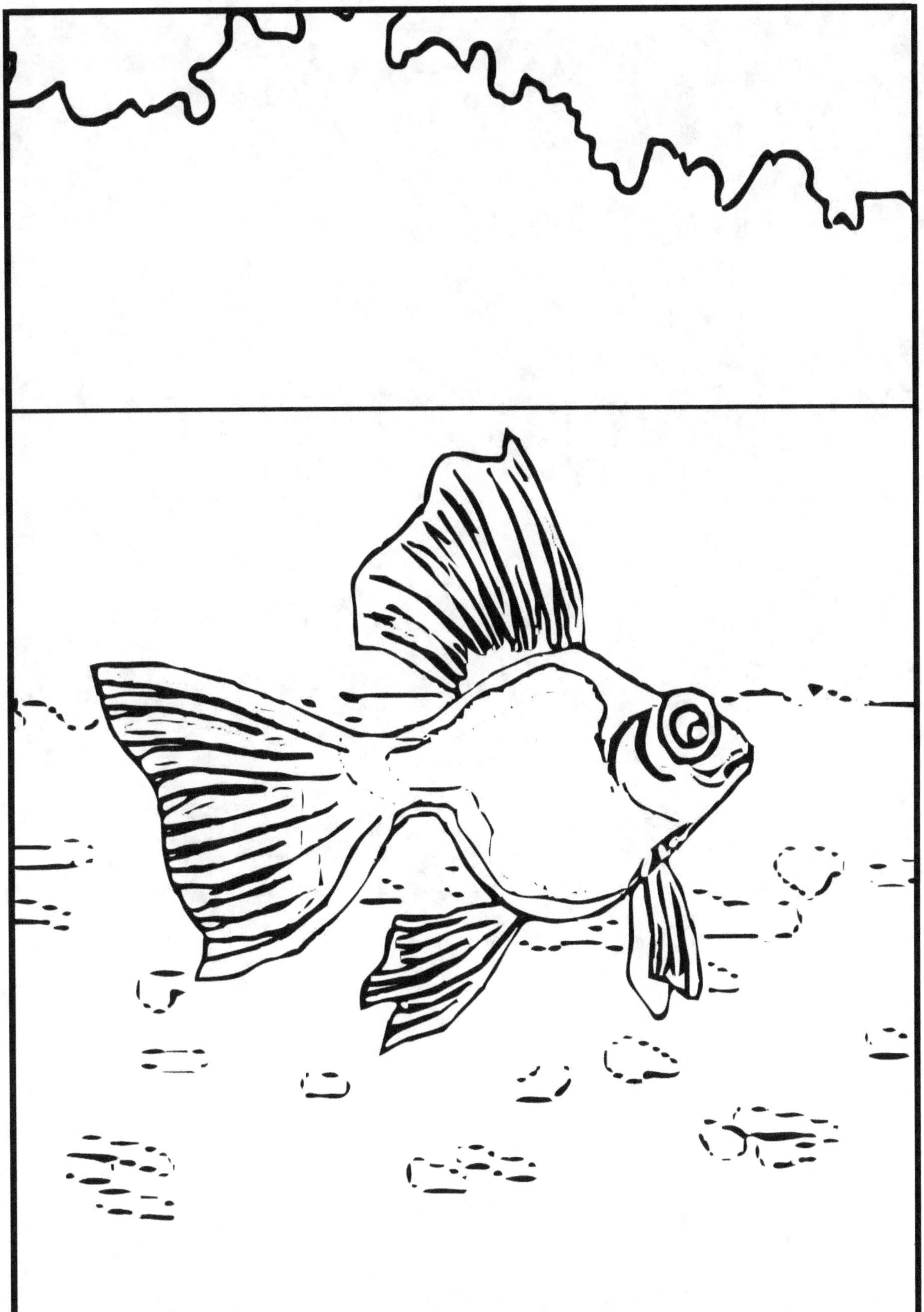

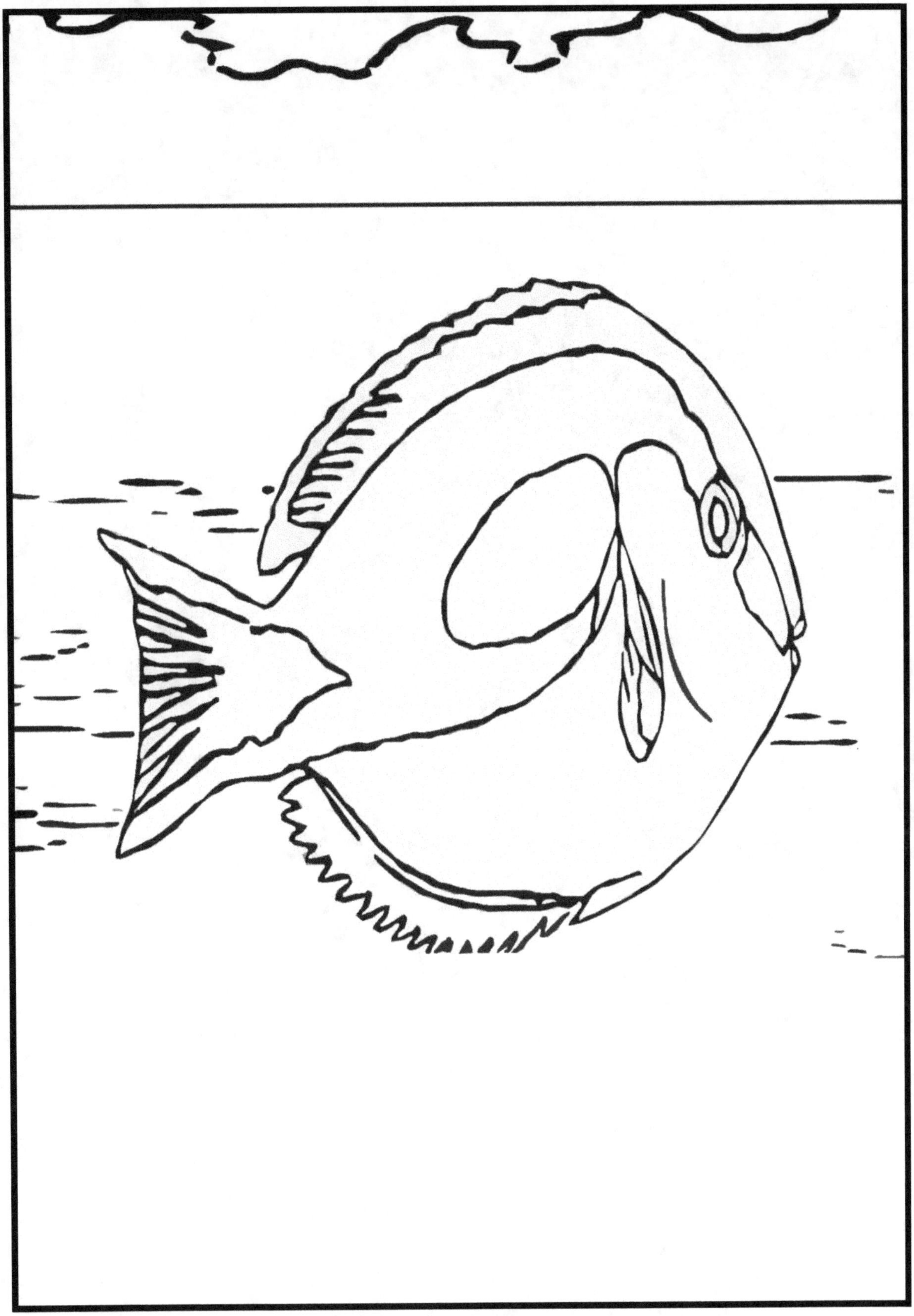

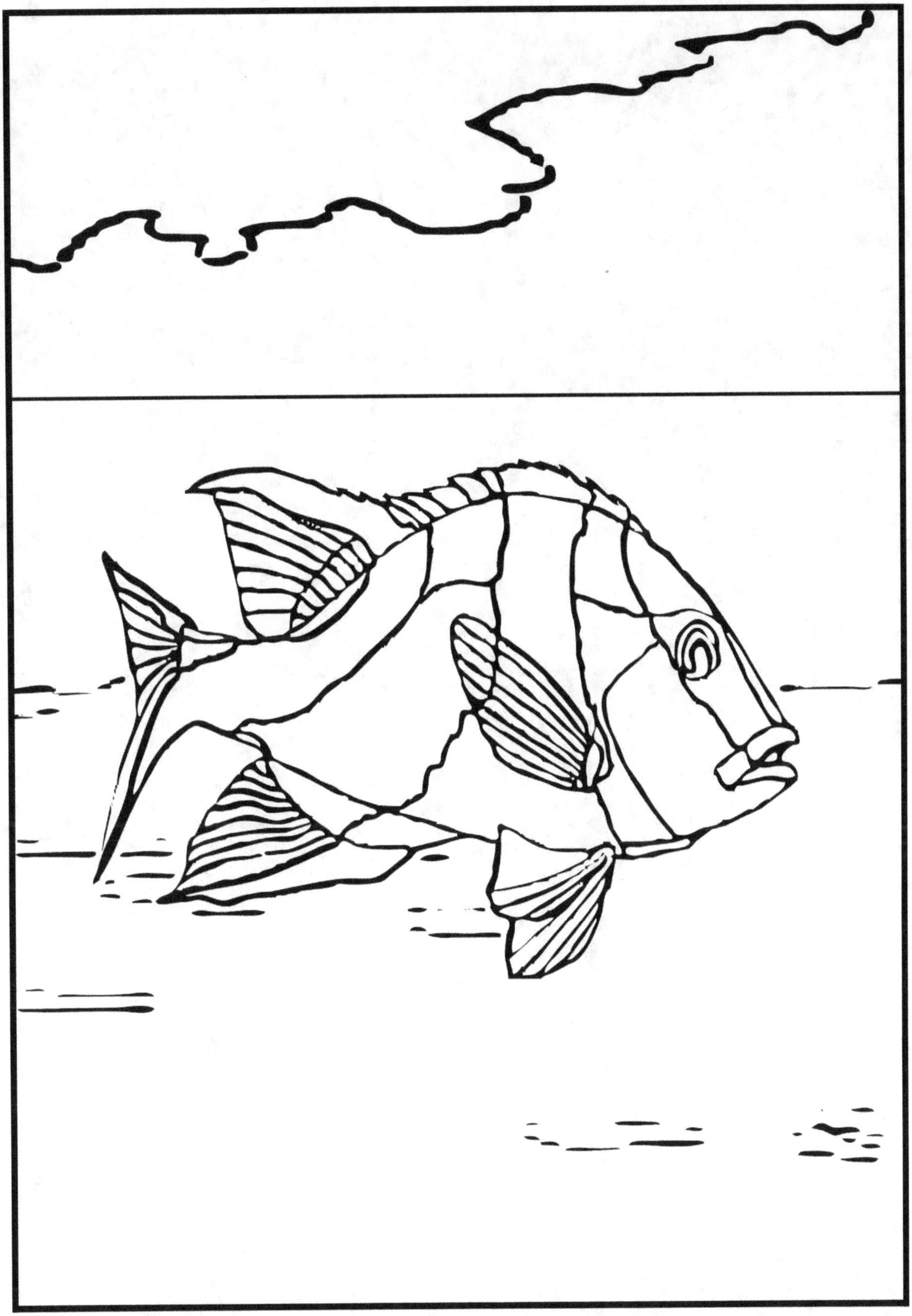

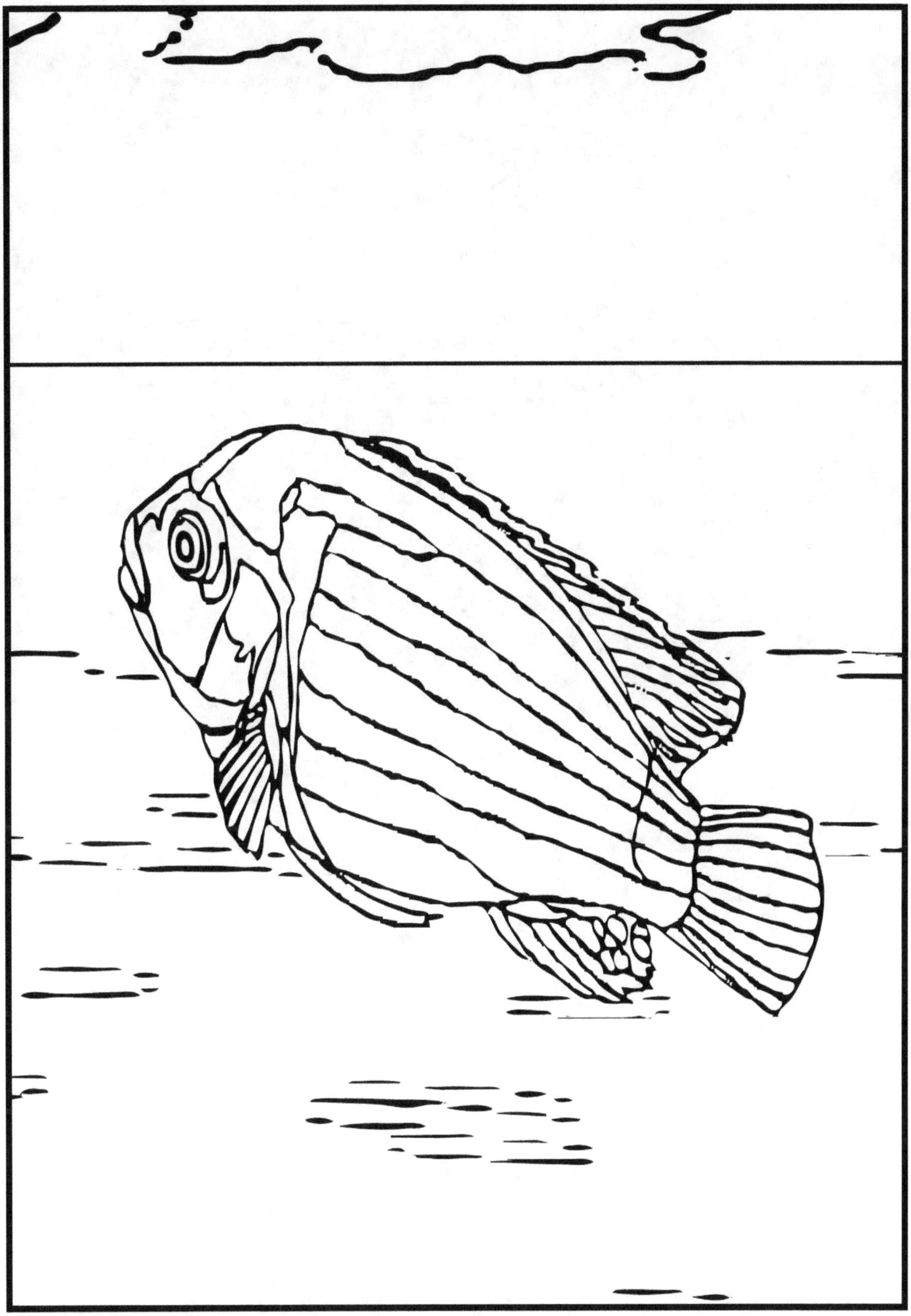

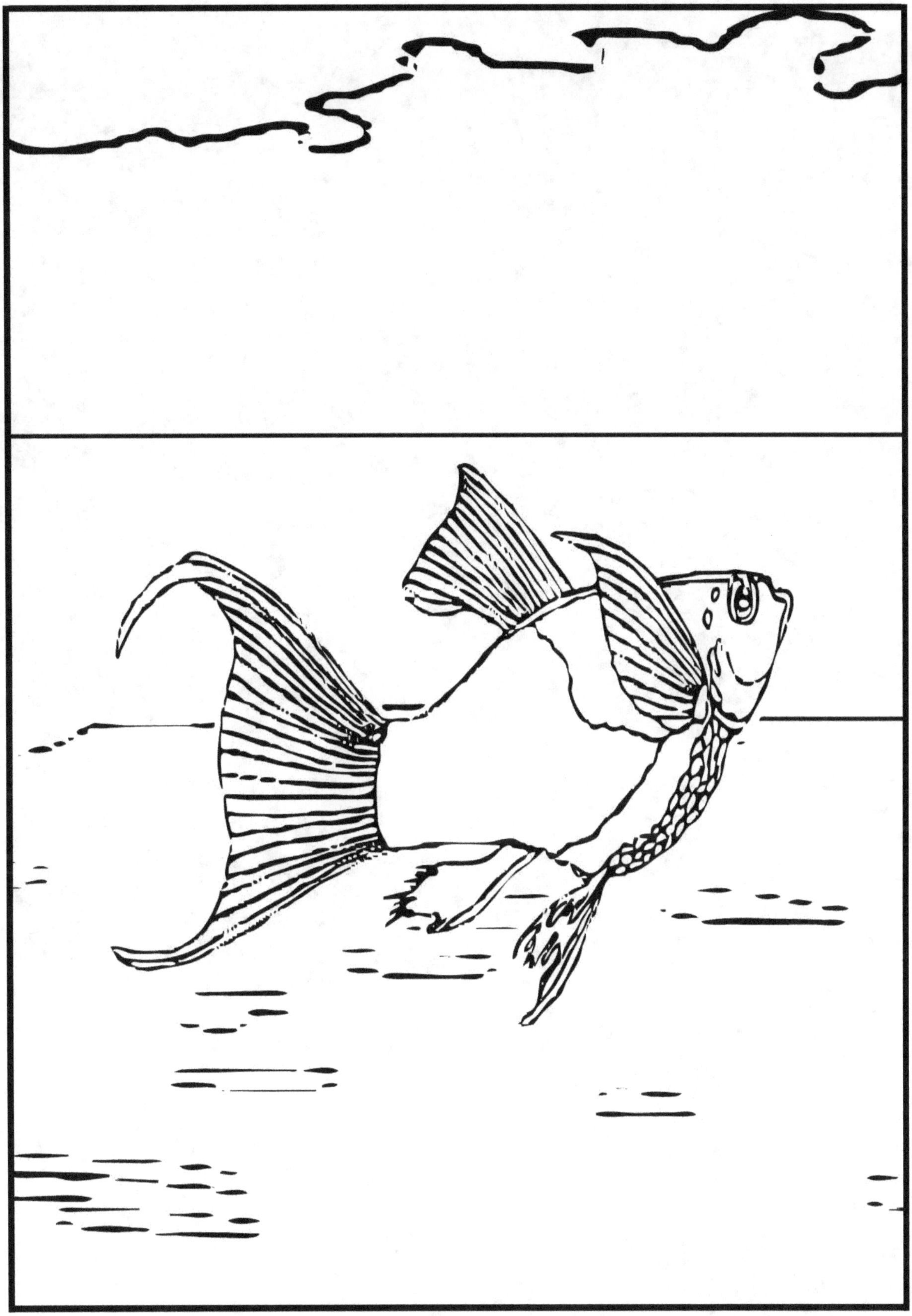

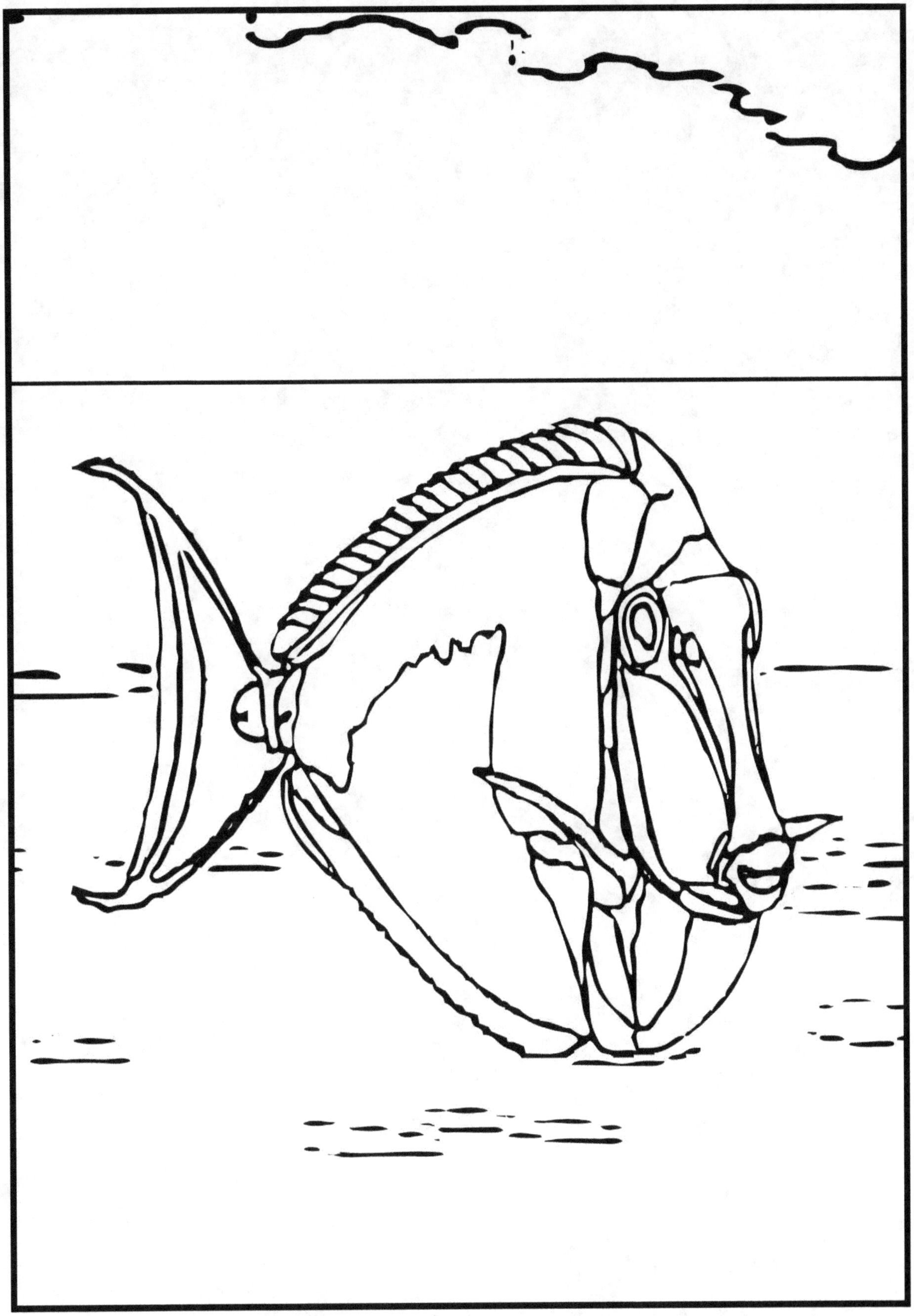

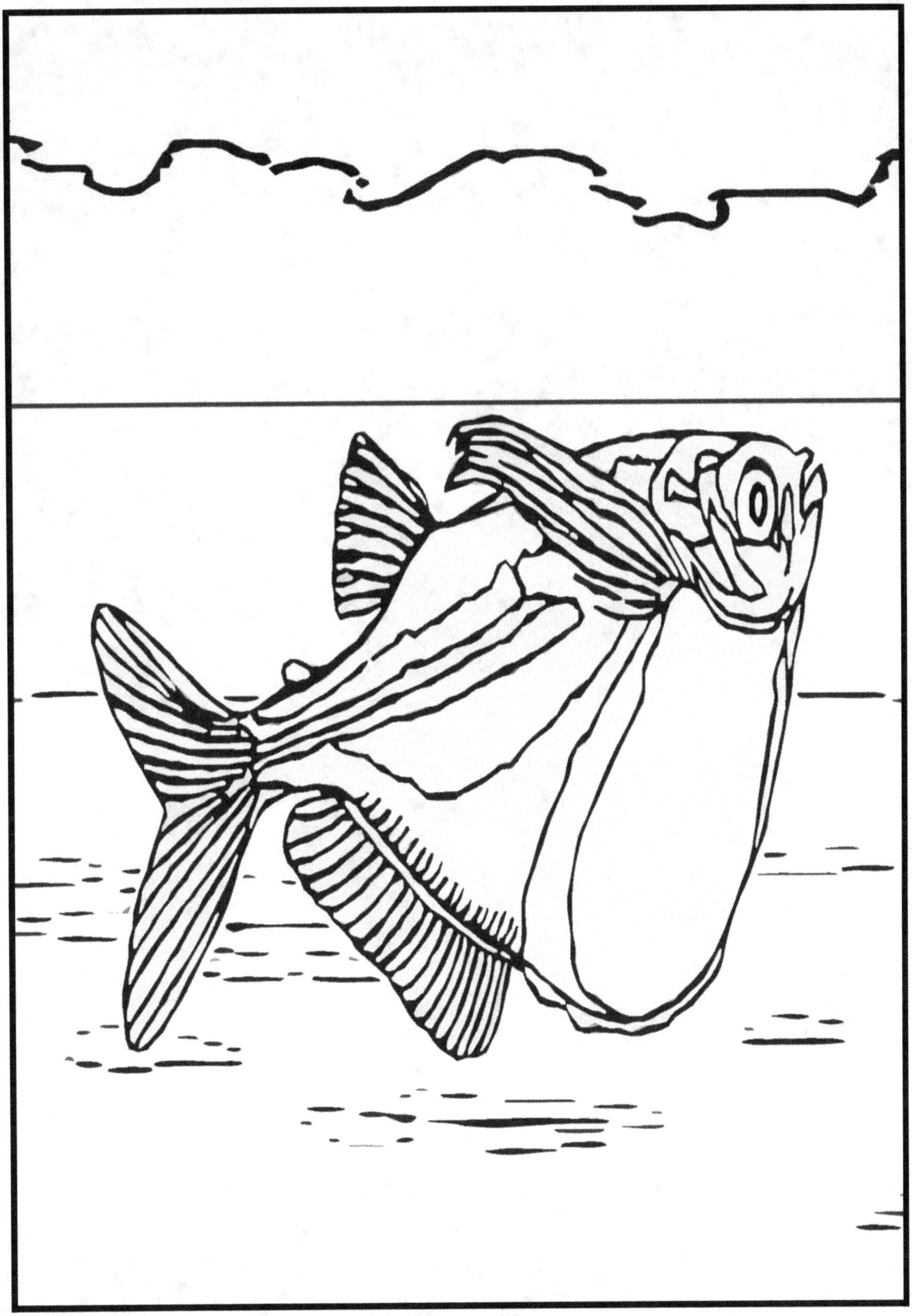

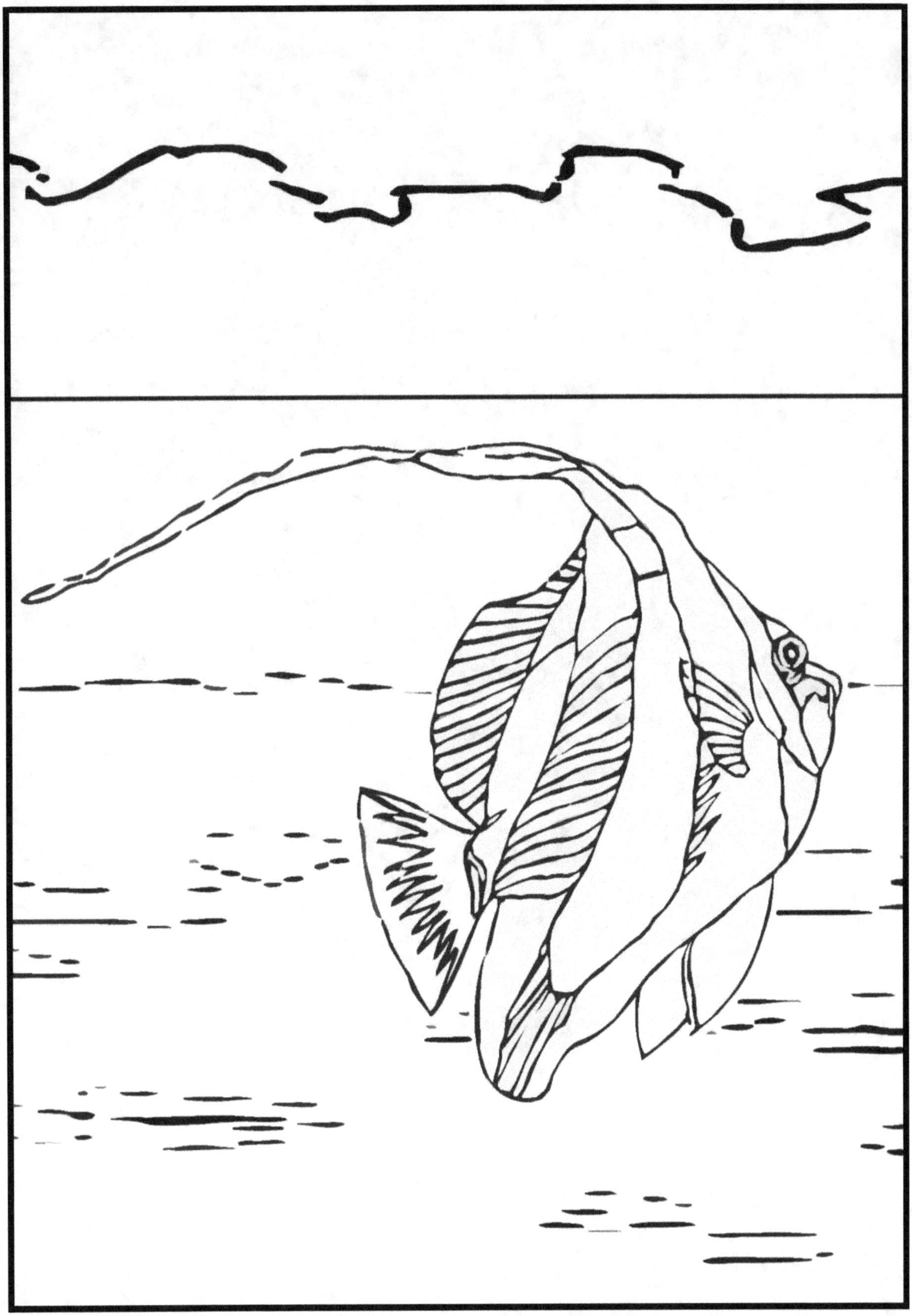

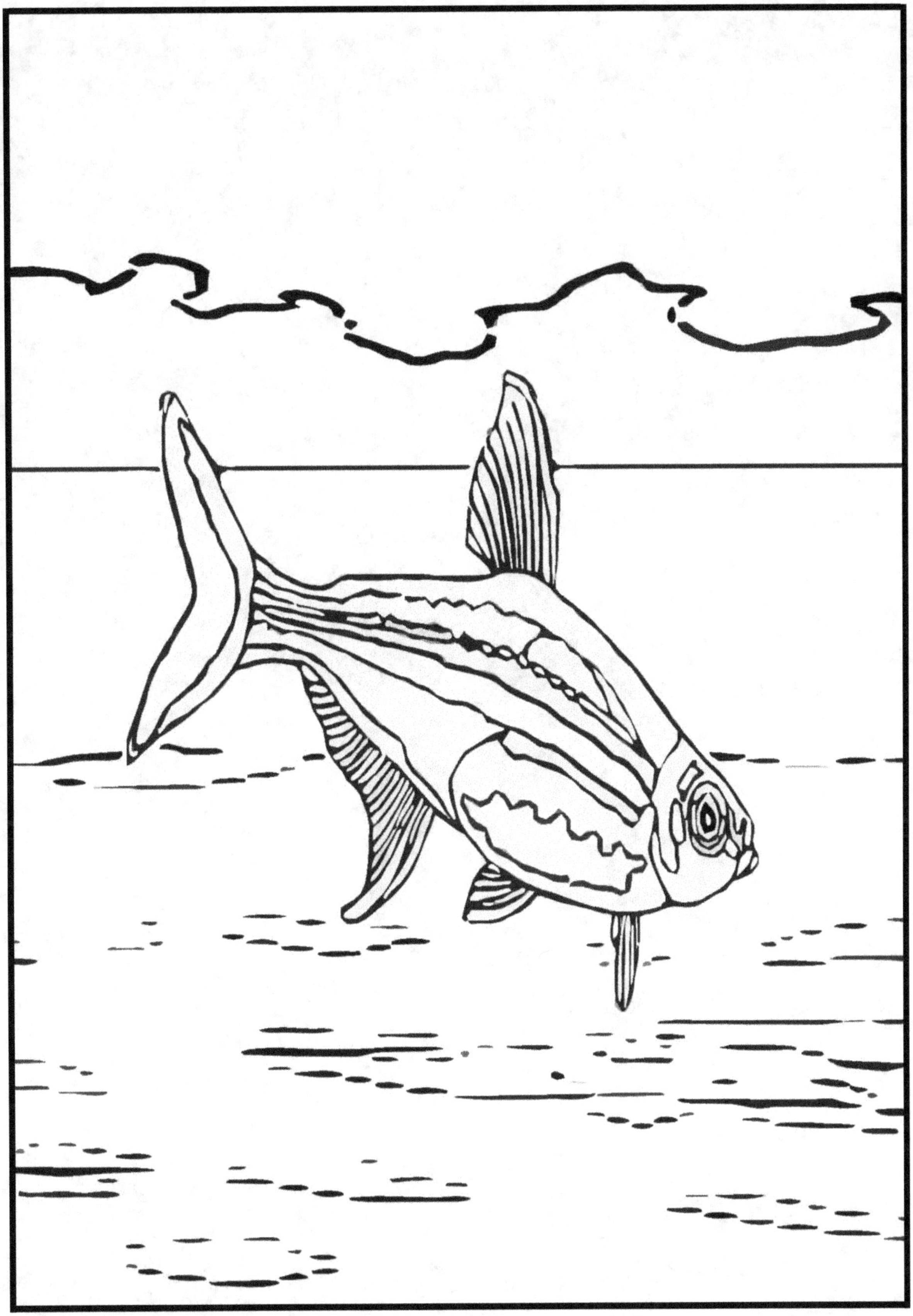

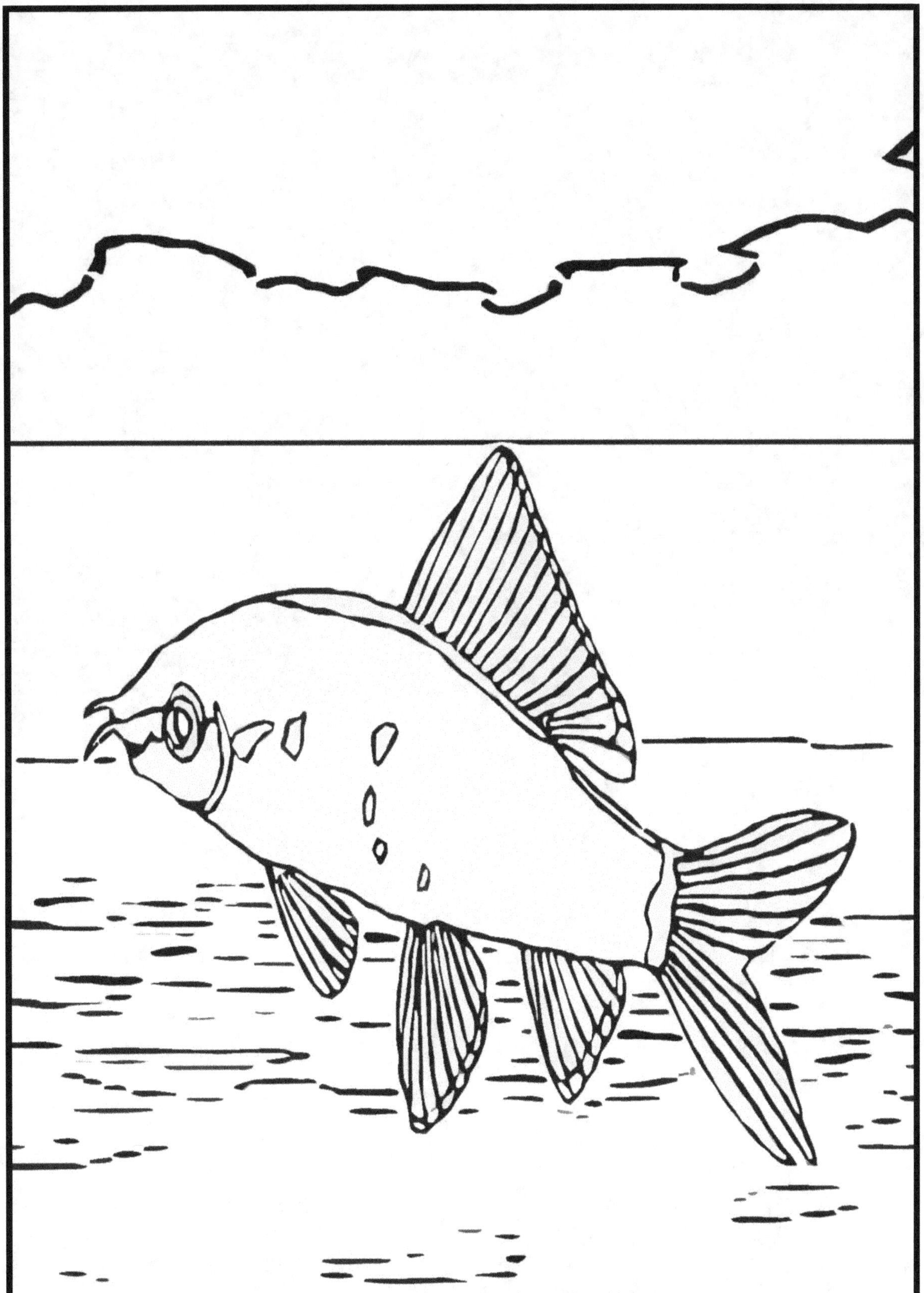

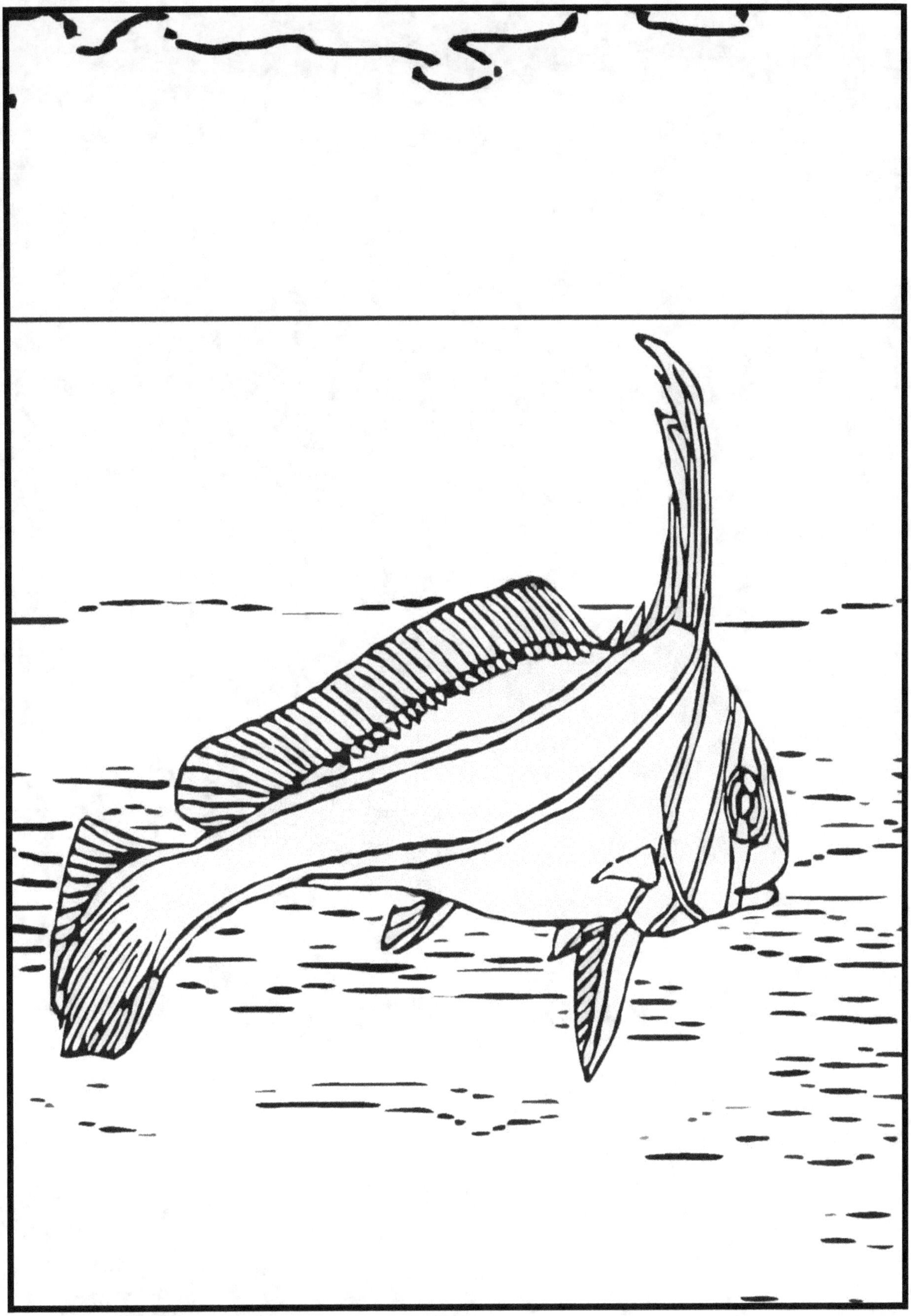

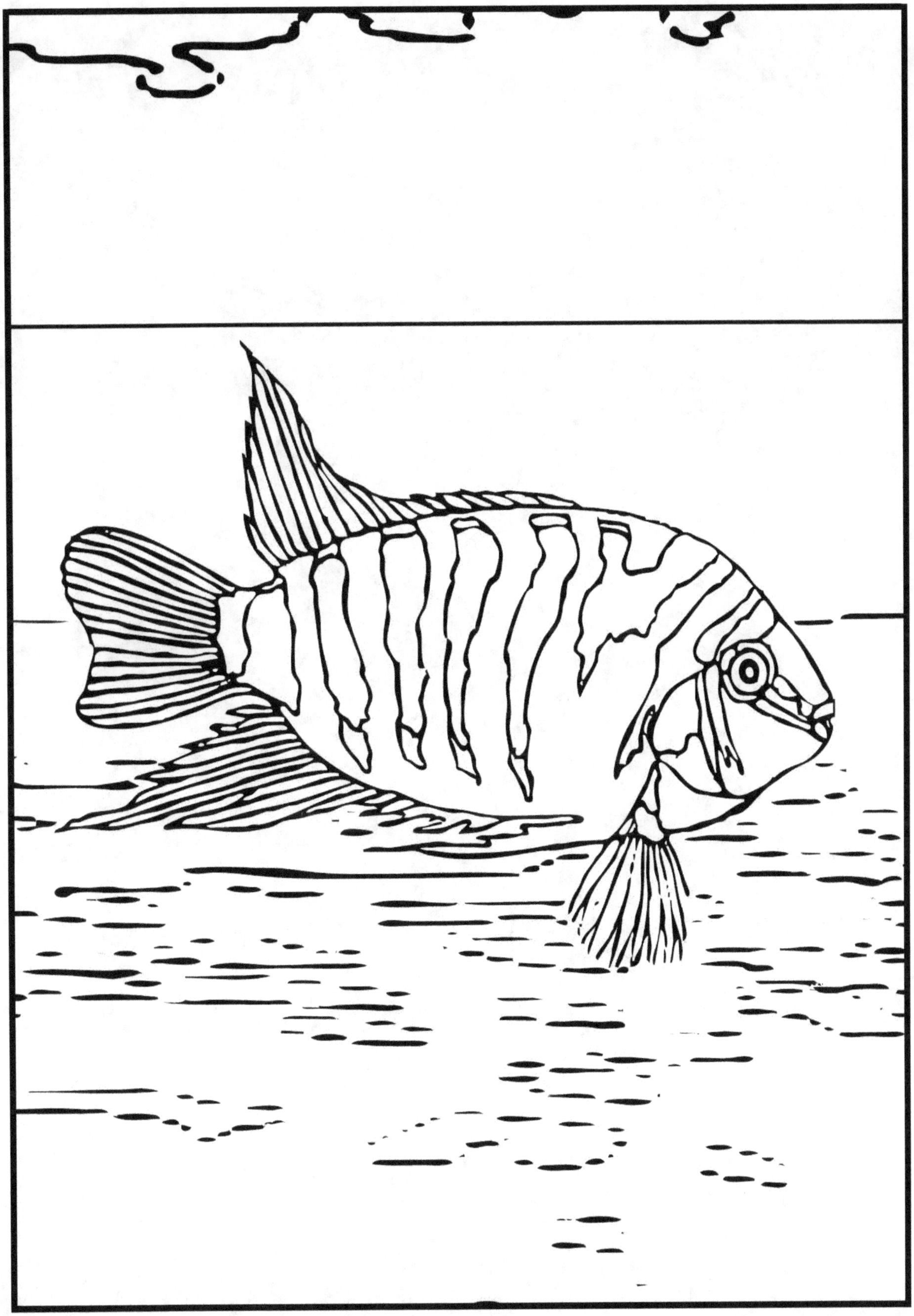

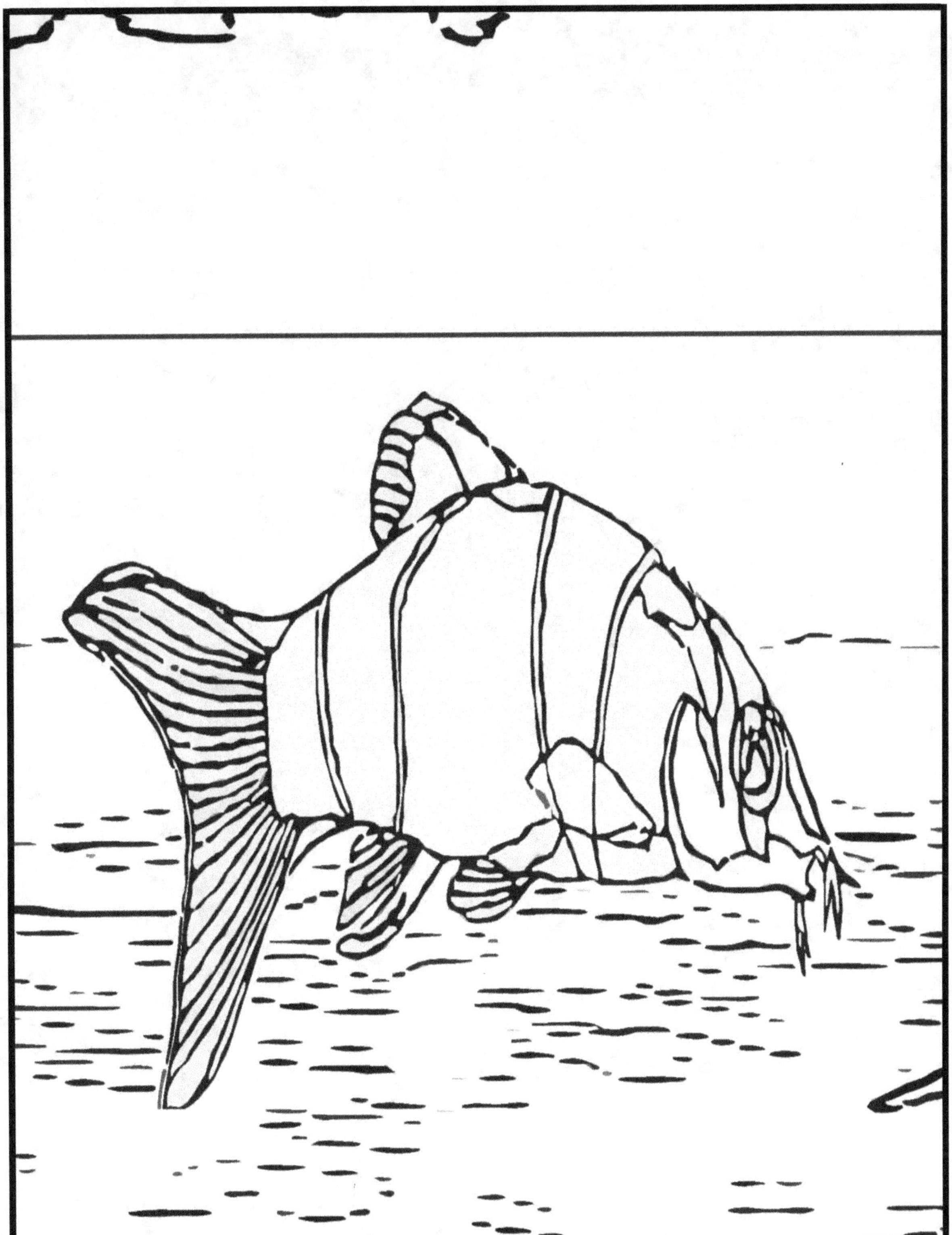

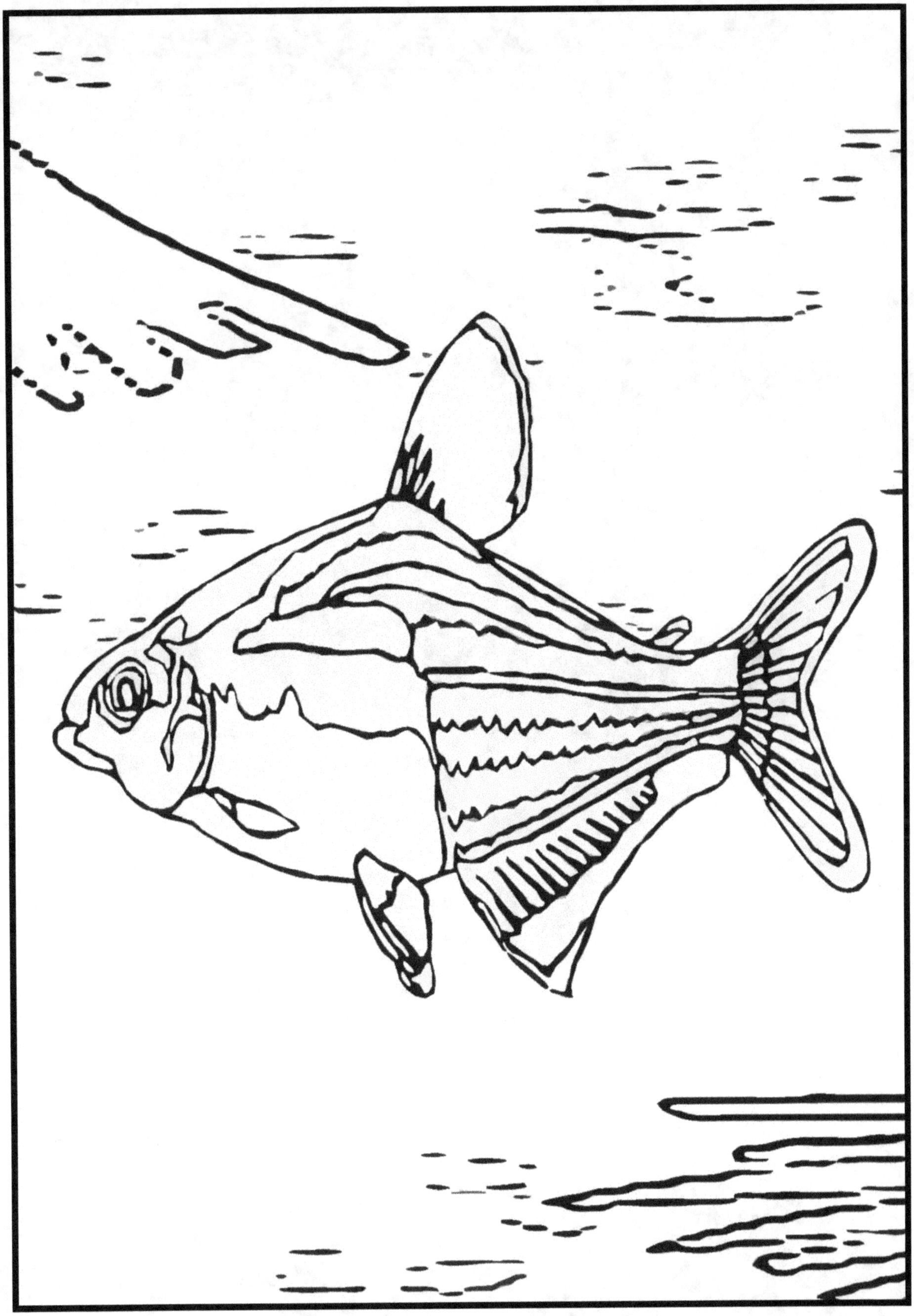

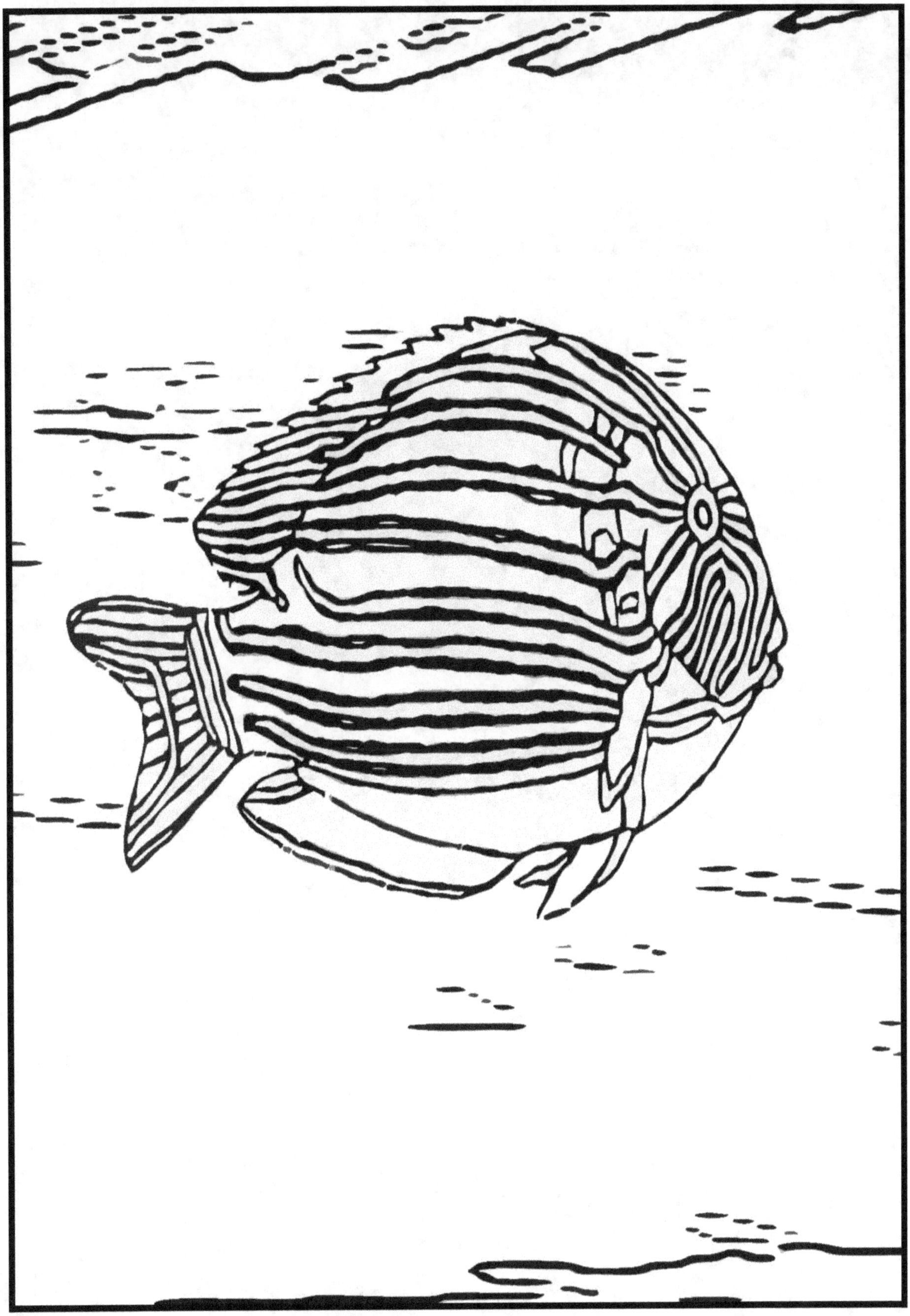

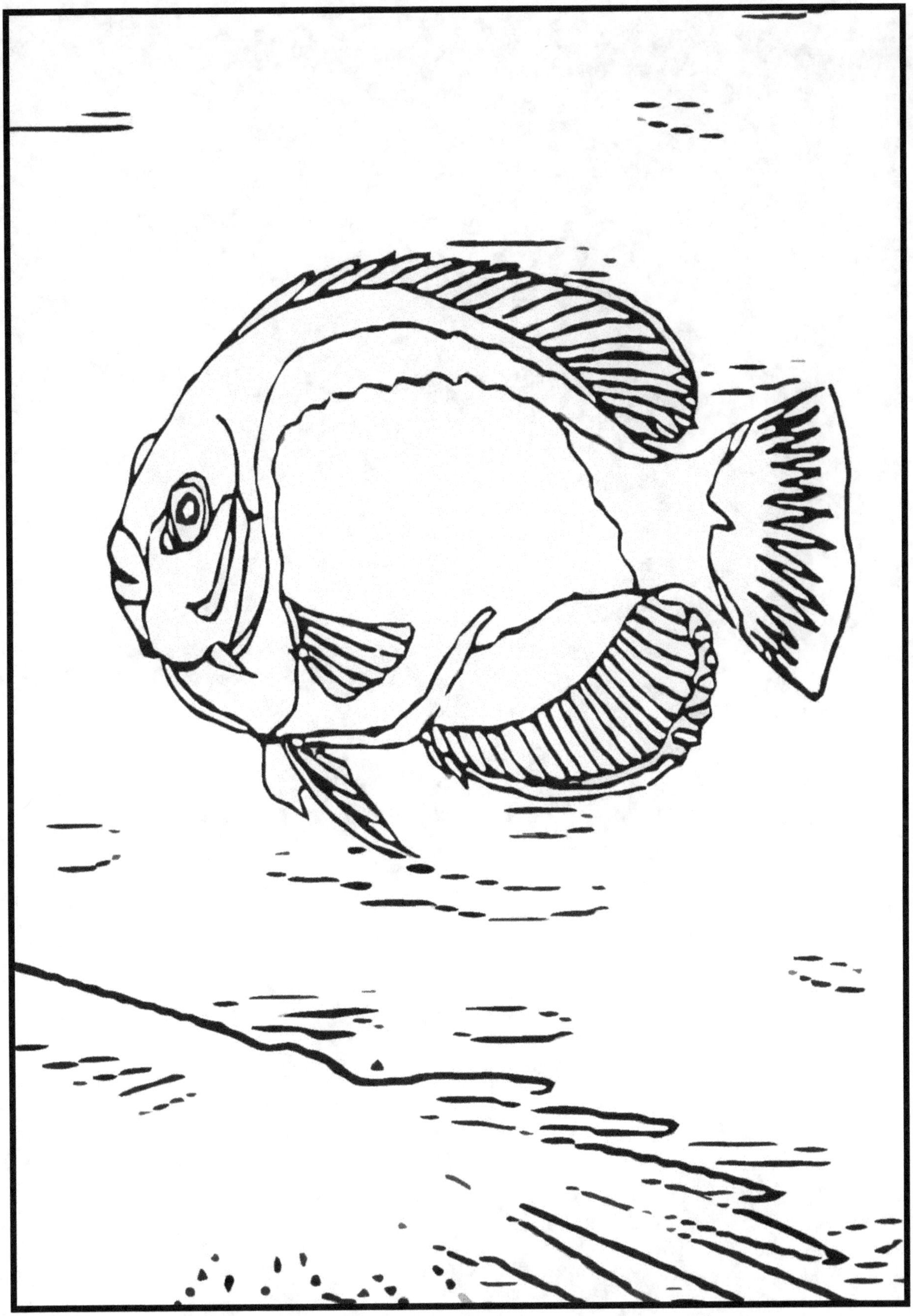

www.ingramcontent.com/pod-product-compliance
Lightning Source LLC
Chambersburg PA
CBHW081310180526
45170CB00007B/2651